KENT
Ghost Stories

Prepare to be frightened by these terrifying tales
from around Kent

By

Richard Holland

BRADWELL
BOOKS

Published by Bradwell Books
9 Orgreave Close Sheffield S13 9NP
Email: books@bradwellbooks.co.uk

British Library Cataloguing in Publication Data: a catalogue
record for this book is available from the British Library.
1st Edition

ISBN: 9781909914056

Print: Gomer Press, Llandysul, Ceredigion SA44 4JL

Design by: jenksdesign@yahoo.co.uk
Photograph Credits: ShutterStock and R. Holland

CONTENTS

The famous White Cliffs of Dover, gateway to one of the most historic and haunted counties in England. Shutterstock/MARKABOND

INTRODUCTION

It would be hard to imagine a more historic county than Kent. It was here that the Romans, the Saxons and the Normans first made landfall at the start of their successful invasions of the islands of Britain. It is quite possible that it was in what is now Kent that prehistoric man first wandered across the land bridge that millennia ago stretched across the English Channel.

Kent is also one of the first places where Christianity – or to be more precise the version of the Christian faith headed by the Church of Rome – became adopted. Canterbury Cathedral is the country's oldest and its archbishop has been the head of first the Catholic and later the Anglican faith in Britain for more than a thousand years. Thanks to its proximity with the continent, Kent has seen historic battles and skirmishes galore and is possessed of some of the finest castles to be found anywhere. There are also many grand and beautiful old stately homes, a good number of which are open to the public.

Kent has another rich heritage – its haunted heritage. The county's ghosts date from periods throughout its long history. Here can be found ghostly Romans, spectral Saxons, medieval knights and ladies, and phantoms from the Tudor and Elizabethan periods, the 18th and 19th centuries and one or two dating from the Second World War. Kent even has a few 'celebrity' ghosts, including Admiral Lord Nelson and Charles Dickens.

These ghosts can be found in many beautiful and historic places, for Kent's towns and villages are among the most picturesque in England. Others haunt those splendid stately homes, castles and other sites of historic interest mentioned above. Still others may be encountered on the winding roads that lead through its charming countryside. There are even phantom ships to be spotted, just out to sea.

The ghostly heritage of Kent is well worth exploring, not only because the stories are so fascinating but because those haunted sites that are open to the public are so rewarding of a visit. I hope you enjoy this ramble through one of the most historic and haunted counties in England.

Richard Holland

A writer of great ghost stories himself, it is perhaps ironic that the ghost of Charles Dickens is among the many said to be encountered in Kent

CREEPS IN CANTERBURY

Canterbury is named after the Canti or Cantiaci, the Celtic tribe who occupied the place at the time of the Roman invasion. It is far and away one of the UK's most historic cities, its picturesque streets and ancient buildings creating a wonderfully 'olde worlde' atmosphere.

Canterbury Cathedral is arguably Britain's oldest. It was founded by St Augustine, the first missionary to be sent by a Pope of Rome to the British Isles. Perhaps to his surprise, he found a church already existed, St Martin's, because the local monarch's queen was herself a Christian. St Martin's is the oldest church in Britain still in use but the cathedral was founded soon after Augustine's arrival, a few years before AD 600. Nothing survives of this Saxon cathedral. The mighty edifice we see today was begun shortly after the Norman Conquest and added to repeatedly up until about the year 1500.

Canterbury Cathedral remains the seat of the leader of the Church of England and is at the centre of the worldwide Anglican community. The Archbishop of Canterbury was the most powerful clergyman in England both before and after Henry VIII's rejection of Roman Catholicism in the 16th century. One of the most dramatic incidents to take place in Canterbury was the murder of Thomas Becket, archbishop during the reign of Henry II. The king and the archbishop had clashed frequently, and when Henry, in frustration cried out, 'Who will rid me of this turbulent priest?' (or words to that effect), several of his knights took it upon themselves to assassinate Becket. They did so in the cathedral itself, which sent shockwaves across Europe. Henry II had to do severe penance, although it's unlikely he ever sanctioned the murder. Becket became a martyr and Canterbury Cathedral the most important place of pilgrimage in medieval England (hence Chaucer's *Canterbury Tales*). The knights who slew Becket became outcasts. We shall encounter more than one of them in ghostly form later on in this book.

It is not Thomas Becket but a later archbishop who haunts Canterbury Cathedral. This is Simon Sudbury, who was killed by poll tax protestors in 1381. His torso was interred in the walls of the cathedral, while his head was buried near his family home in Suffolk. His apparition has not been seen for

Magnificent Canterbury Cathedral has several ghosts.
© *Shutterstock/Kamira*

many years but was described as being of 'a dignified character with a grey beard and a fair complexion'.

Phantom monks have also been seen in the cathedral, both in the crypt and in the cloisters. John Hippisley tells of a recent encounter in the cloisters in his *Haunted Canterbury*. A security guard spotted a group of what he took to be schoolboys dressed in monkish habits. When he asked them what they were doing there they replied in unison: 'We are for the Scriptorium!' After this oddly Harry Potter moment the guard let them go on their way, but when he mentioned the incident to his supervisor, he was reminded that it was way past most boys' bedtime and was also informed that Canterbury Cathedral's Scriptorium (a room for writing books and manuscripts) burnt down in the 12th century. Eighty monks perished in the blaze.

A secular ghost is that of 'Nell', a servant who would wait upon the cathedral clergy and had the misfortune to fall in love with a canon. The object of her devotion made it clear to Nell that he could not return her affection, for his life was committed to God. The girl respected his purity, so one can only imagine her shock and sense of betrayal when she entered the canon's chamber to clean it and found him in bed with another woman. The sight drove her out of her mind and in a frenzy of grief and rage she killed both the canon and his companion. Nell was hanged for the crime and her body buried near the door which leads from the cathedral to the attached King's School.

In his *Haunted Places of Kent*, Rupert Matthews describes Nell's ghost as 'a most disturbing phantom'. He writes: 'The pretty features of the girl are distorted by grief and anguish, turning to anger and hatred. Those who see it are guaranteed to suffer a death in the family within a year and a day of seeing the ghost, or so it is said.'

Among the other haunted historic sites in Canterbury highlighted by John Hippisley is the **Westgate Tower**, a massive stone structure set up after the original wooden gate was destroyed during the Peasants' Revolt of 1381. In later years the Westgate was used as a prison and its ghost seems

The Westgate Tower in Canterbury, where a council worker had a distinctly spooky experience. Shutterstock/ Jaime Pharr

to date from that period. One evening a council worker in the Westgate was just about to leave for the day when he found he had somehow been locked in. Suddenly the atmosphere grew unbearably cold and the man then heard an eerie sound as if several people were dragging a body down the staircase on the right-hand side of the tower. The steps descended past the room in which the witness was locked in, down into the stairwell. At that moment the door was found not to be locked after all, and the council worker made his escape. He wondered afterwards whether he had heard the ghostly echo of some unfortunate being dragged to his execution.

Sudbury Tower in Pound Lane is another location said to be haunted by Simon Sudbury, after whom the building is named. That at least is the identity given to the ghostly gent with the 'greying square-cut beard' who has been seen here. Tradition has it that it was in the **Archbishop's Old Palace**, now part of the King's School, that the four knights who murdered Thomas Becket met before making their fatal journey to the cathedral. One of the four, thought to be the ringleader, Reginald Fitz-Urse, reappears in the Old Palace on the anniversary of the murder, 29 December. On the same date the neighing and stamping of invisible horses is said to be heard under the tower of **St Thomas's Church**, a ghostly re-enactment of Becket's killers fleeing the scene of the crime.

In the ancient **St Thomas's Hospital**, founded to cater for all the pilgrims flocking to Canterbury after Becket's martyrdom, a phantom monk continues to pray in the undercroft. He is seen at dusk and has made his appearance, off and on, for four centuries. The ghosts of hooded Franciscan monks are also to be seen in and around **Greyfriars Chapel**, all that remains of a 13th-century friary on the site. Spectral soldiers have been glimpsed among the ruins of **Canterbury Castle**. Their shadowy forms are too vague to determine clearly which period in history they date from but it's possible they are the shades of Royalists who vainly fought to defend the city from the advance of the Parliamentarians during the Civil War.

The final Canterbury ghost I'd like to mention was reported by Rupert Matthews. This is the 'cycling Mayor'. According to Matthews, a 19th-century Mayor of Canterbury found the quickest way to get round his city was to cycle everywhere, something considered rather eccentric in his day. Today, this two-wheeled spook is still to be seen, 'darting down the narrow streets … usually in the winter'.

The Greyfriars Chapel is haunted by the shades of monks who formerly lived and prayed at the Franciscan Friary that was founded here.
Shutterstock/ Paco Lozano

WRAITHS IN ROCHESTER

The ancient and handsome town – formerly city – of Rochester is now part of the unitary authority of Medway and is another of Kent's gems. It is dominated by two medieval edifices: its cathedral and its castle. Both are haunted.

The ghost of **Rochester Castle** dates from the 13th-century conflict between King Henry III and the powerful baron Simon de Montfort, Earl of Leicester, who sought to curb the monarch's absolute power over his subjects. A romantic legend tells of a kind of *ménage à trois* in the midst of battle. Simon de Montfort's forces laid siege to the castle in 1264. In charge of defending the castle was a crusader, Ralph de Capo. His betrothed, the lovely Lady Blanche de Warrene, was in residence at the time. And the man she threw over for de Capo, a knight named Gilbert de Clare, was one of the commanders of the besieging force.

Rochester Castle survived the siege. When it was lifted, Ralph de Capo gathered some of his best knights and rode out to hunt down any stragglers from de Montfort's besiegers. Gilbert de Clare took the opportunity to disguise himself in a suit of armour resembling de Capo's and he sneaked into the castle in search of the woman who had jilted him. He found Lady Blanche on the battlements and began to reprimand her brutally. Lady Blanche's new lover happened to glance over his shoulder and saw her being manhandled by the mysterious knight. A skilled archer, de Capo immediately grabbed a bow and let fly an arrow at the

KENT
Ghost Stories

troublemaker. His aim was true but – alas! – the arrow glanced off de Clare's armour and pierced Lady Blanche's heart.

'That same night,' writes veteran ghost-hunter Peter Underwood, 'her ghost walked the battlements in a white robe, her raven hair streaming in the breeze, the fatal arrow still embedded in her bosom, and on the anniversary of the tragedy she is still said to haunt the battlements of the old castle, bewailing the sad fate of having been killed by her lover.'

Underwood also notes that 'unexplained footsteps' have been heard in the round tower below Rochester Castle's mighty keep. An alternative version of the legend states that it was here that de Capo found his beloved Blanche struggling in the arms of de Clare and where the fatal accident occurred.

Rochester Cathedral is England's second oldest, having been founded in AD 604 by Bishop Justus. The current building dates from soon after the Norman Conquest, with later medieval additions. It underwent a major restoration in 1872. The great Victorian novelist Charles Dickens had hoped to be buried at Rochester Cathedral. Dickens spent many years in Rochester and used the town as the basis for many locations in his books. As a boy he coveted a grand house named Gads Hill Place. When fame and fortune were his, he purchased Gads Hill Place and moved in, to his great satisfaction. On his death, it was decided so great a man should be interred in Poets Corner, Westminster Abbey, rather than at Rochester. Perhaps it is his disappointment at not having his wishes met, despite the honour accorded him,

The round tower in the foreground is considered one of the most haunted parts of Rochester Castle. © English Heritage

that has led to the ghost of Dickens allegedly being seen in the cathedral's burial ground.

A few years after his death in June 1870, there came reports of Dickens's ghost appearing under the 'moon-faced clock' on the **Corn Exchange** building, as immortalised in *The Mystery of Edwin Drood*. It has now entered local folklore that the ghost manifests at Christmas time in this spot just as the clock strikes twelve.

The Corn Exchange was built with money provided by Sir Cloudesley Shovell, an Admiral of the Fleet who became MP for Rochester in 1698. He also paid for the elaborate plasterwork on the ceiling of the **Guildhall**. For many years after his death in a shipwreck off the Isles of Scilly in 1707, Sir Cloudesley's ghost was seen strolling through various parts of the Guildhall, in his splendid naval uniform. Today he is rarely seen but people have reported doors opening and closing by themselves and the feeling of a presence pushing past them in the corridors, suggesting that the ghost is still wandering about nonetheless.

The graveyard at Rochester's handsome Norman cathedral is said to be haunted by the spirit of Charles Dickens. Shutterstock/ MARKABOND

DOVER SOULS

When the inventory known as the *Domesday Book* was compiled twenty years after the Norman Conquest the port of Dover was listed first above all other entries, even London. Its significance as a strategically important location, so close to the continent of Europe, was recognised by the Romans before the Normans and echoed as late as the 1940s in the Second World War anthem 'The White Cliffs of Dover'.

The keep or Great Tower may be the most haunted part of Dover Castle
© *English Heritage*

Dover Castle is the most visible symbol of its former importance as a defensive site. The history of the site is a long one. The Romans took over an existing Iron Age hill fort and built a lighthouse here. The lighthouse is still standing and is one of the best preserved in Europe. Beside it is a Saxon church, all that remains of a settlement which was rapidly developed into a wooden and earthwork fort by William the Conqueror. The stone castle wasn't begun until the 1160s.

Dover Castle remains one of the most impressive in England. It is dominated by its massive keep, 83 feet (25m) high. Also known as the Great Tower, it was built by Henry II immediately after he carried out his penance for the murder of Thomas Becket at Canterbury Cathedral. It is a commanding symbol of kingly

From the top floor down to the cellars, Dover Castle is haunted on every level
© *English Heritage*

authority but far more than just a military stronghold: it was used as a regional palace where Henry could show off and entertain his nobles and foreign dignitaries in high style. Subsequent Plantagenet kings continued to add to Dover Castle's strength and magnificence, and over the centuries it has hosted numerous royal visits by, among others, Henry VIII and Elizabeth I. The castle remained continuously garrisoned for 800 years, until 1958.

With so much history attached to so important a place, it would be disappointing indeed if Dover Castle did not have its ghosts. Fortunately, it is very haunted indeed. The best-known ghost of Dover Castle is the headless drummer boy who patrols its outer walls. Tradition has it the drummer boy dates from the period of the Napoleonic Wars. Napoleon's forces were massed on the opposite side of the English Channel, so close they could be seen on clear days from Dover's battlements. Attempted invasion seemed inevitable.

Dover Castle was on high alert and the young drummer was one of many tasked with patrolling the walls and keeping a lookout for boats or ships at sea. After dark, all English boats would be in harbour, meaning that any out at sea were likely to be French. If the boy spotted a sail, he was to drum the alert.

One morning the drummer boy failed to report in after his night on duty. After a search, his brutally battered and decapitated body was found at the foot of the wall. He had presumably been silenced for something he had seen or overheard, but as no one was ever apprehended for his murder, the reason for it was never discovered. The boy's headless phantom, his drum by his side, began to be seen soon after the murder, and is said to walk the battlements on dark, moonless nights.

The aforementioned Great Tower appears to be the most haunted part of the castle. The Red Lady haunts the Great Hall and is one of the most frequently seen ghosts at Dover Castle. Dressed in the long, red gown that has suggested her name, she floats down from the vaulting in the eastern corner of the hall. This may be the same apparition that has been seen peering out of an upper floor window. A particularly dashing phantom has been encountered on the ground floor. He is described by Rupert Matthews, in his *Haunted Places of Kent*, as 'A richly dressed gentleman in 17th-century outfit. Equipped with knee-high riding boots and swathed in a richly purple cloak, [he] is topped off by a wide-brimmed hat adorned with a dramatic plume.' Known simply as 'the Cavalier', the ghost strides about as if he owns the place, even strolling through solid walls as if they were of no consequence.

The spectre in the King's Bedroom is invisible above the waist: only the lower half of the torso is seen walking through the room. This is disturbing enough, but several visitors and members of staff have also reported a feeling of extreme unease in the chamber even when nothing is seen. One described the 'horrid feeling' as being as if 'there was a man in there causing torment and death'. Unable to stand the sensation, she hurried out of the room as soon as she could.

A horrible story is told about Peverell's Tower, one of the oldest parts of Dover Castle. It is named after William de Peverell, who was tasked with the early construction of the stone castle in the 12th century. Peverell appointed a fellow Norman, called Geoffrey, to oversee the work, but he was a poor manager and accidents kept happening. After a fall of masonry killed a workman, the builders went on strike (allegedly the first strike in English history!). Peverell was furious and, rather than accepting that the fault was his for failing to provide scaffolding as he had been urged to do, he threw all the stonemasons into prison.

Just then an old woman came on the scene. She was a daily visitor to the building site, selling food to the workers, and she always brought her little black dog with her. On spotting her dog, Geoffrey suggested that the best way to put an end to all the 'bad luck' would be to perform an animal sacrifice. Borrowed from the Romans, this was a much more common practice in the Middle Ages than you might suppose. Peverell agreed and demanded that the old woman hand over her dog so he could 'immure' it in the walls.

Naturally, the poor old soul refused. Peverell insisted and when the woman continued to cling on to her pet, he walled her up, too. The unfortunate woman's screams for mercy could be heard behind the masonry for days, and the dog's howls for more than a week. This horrendous deed did nothing to make up for Geoffrey's incompetence and he fell to his death from the tower shortly before completion. William de Peverell died not long after. Some said their deaths were the result of the old woman's angry spirit. Today the shades of the old woman and her dog are still said to be seen in the vicinity of Peverell's Tower and the howling of a dog is occasionally heard emanating from it.

Below the keep, in the rock that supports it, a network of tunnels and chambers has been created. They are thought to have originally been dug out by the Romans but have been used and extended by a succession of occupants. During the Second World War, armed services personnel retreated to the depths of the tunnels to escape the almost constant bombardment from the Luftwaffe and long-range artillery based across the Channel in France. Two ghosts dating from this period have been encountered in the tunnels, in the area where a wartime hospital was established. One is a soldier dressed in khaki; the other is a young nurse. Ghostly voices of two men in conversation in the Dynamo Room have rather optimistically been identified as those of Winston Churchill and Admiral Ramsay discussing the Dunkirk evacuation.

A '17th-century pikeman' and the apparition of a man sporting a blue cloak have also been reported from the tunnels. The latter may well be the Cavalier known to haunt the keep's above-ground rooms.

A couple of American tourists had a weird experience at the outlying St John's Tower, according to Andrew Green. They heard 'realistic screams and moans' coming from behind the tower's massive cylindrical walls. They assumed the grim sounds were tape recordings intended to create a bit of atmosphere for visitors and must have gone rather pale when they were informed by a puzzled guide that no such recordings were used at the castle.

There is one other haunted site at Dover Castle. This is the ancient tower that stands beside the old church. During the

The remains of a Roman lighthouse survives near the original Saxon church in Dover Castle. A mysterious figure in white has been seen here. © English Heritage

Saxon period, the structure was used as a bell tower but had started life as a *pharos*, or lighthouse, to guide Roman ships into harbour. The ghostly figure in white glimpsed from time to time near the old lighthouse is thought by some to be that of a Roman dressed in a toga.

Beyond the castle there are a number of other haunted locations in and around Dover. In particular, there are the **Western Heights**, highlighted by author Lorraine Sencicle in her book *Haunted Dover*. The Western Heights is the name given to the cliffs which overlook the western side of the town. Many strange tales are told about them. Tradition has it that criminals were punished during the Dark Ages by being thrown over the cliffs to their death. Here the mysterious Knights Templar had a church which became the centre of the now lost village of Braddon. Braddon is believed to be the place where the 14th-century pestilence known as the Black Death first reached England. The plague struck again in 1666 and its victims were buried in a communal pit where Braddon formerly stood. The ghosts of these unlucky villagers are said to still haunt the Heights, an eerie sight shuffling about in their filthy shrouds.

According to Lorraine Sencicle, the Drop Redoubt, an 18th-century fort on the Western Heights, is the haunt of the headless drummer boy, rather than the castle. She states that his name was Peter and that he was murdered for a bag of soldiers' pay he was carrying for the quartermaster.

Another headless ghost haunts the **Market Square**. It is thought to be of William de la Pole, the First Duke of Suffolk, who was beheaded by the French in 1450. His head was buried in St Peter's Church, which formerly stood in Market Square. Even older is the apparition of Archbishop Geoffrey, in full episcopal regalia, who wanders around in the vicinity of Dover College, which stands on the site of a priory where Geoffrey was briefly imprisoned during the reign of Richard I.

One of Dover's most important houses is **Maison Dieu House** in Biggin Street. Dating from 1665, Maison Dieu House was the scene of a dramatic incident when conspirators attempted to assassinate William of Orange when he landed at Dover from Holland prior to being invested as king of England. A servant employed in the house, Mary Gray, got wind of the plot and helped prevent it, but was killed by the conspirators. She now haunts the house.

Several of the caves in those famous White Cliffs were used by smugglers to stash their contraband. Those high up in the cliffs were created by, or at the least enlarged by, the smugglers themselves. One of these, the so-called **Coining House Cave**, was used to store tax-dodged wool from the continent. It is haunted by a government informer named Richard Carter, who made his living exposing smugglers' activities. Carter was lured to the Coining House by a beautiful young woman called Susanne, who then betrayed him to the smugglers. They pushed him out of the cave and he fell 400 feet to his death. Susanne and the rest of the gang were eventually captured by Richard's father, who was also a government agent.

Arguably the weirdest of all Dover's ghosts is the one to be encountered in **Connaught Park**. According to Rupert

Matthews, 'This phantom appears dramatically around dusk, looming up out of the gloom like some dreadful monster, which is a fairly accurate description. Shaped much like a man this ghost towers seven feet tall. Its head is grotesque to say the least. One witness described the apparition as having a dog's head, another that it has a long beak. The monstrously deformed head of this spectre causes alarm and fright, before the ghost vanishes as suddenly as it appeared.'

MORE HAUNTED TOWNS

The three places explored above are by no means the only haunted towns in Kent. **Faversham**, for example, has several. Arden's House, a handsome Tudor town house, was the scene of a shocking crime in 1551. Here Thomas Arden, Mayor of Faversham, was brutally murdered by his wife and her lover. The murder became such a cause célèbre that an Elizabethan tragedy was written about it, *Arden of Feversham* (some have attributed it to Shakespeare). For years the bloodstains which resulted from the slaying stubbornly refused to be washed out. In more recent times mysterious footsteps have been heard in the property, which may or may not be some echo of the crime. The apparition of a monk or priest – presumably entirely unconnected with the murder – has also been seen.

Ghostly footsteps also haunt Faversham's attractive Guildhall. They are heard thumping down the stairs and then pacing into the Council Chamber. They are so heavy that on one occasion their manifestation was noisy enough to interrupt a council meeting. They were heard by a number of councillors, three of whom vainly went in search of a possible intruder. The pacing continued around the chamber even after the main overhead lights had been switched on to try to find a cause for them. No one knows to whom the footsteps belong.

Faversham's best-known haunted spot is to be found some way outside the town, among the marshes at Hollowshore. This is the venerable Shipwright's Arms, haunted by a sailor whose ship sank in the nearby Swale. More dead than alive, he crawled through the bogs and marshes, fortifying himself with a bottle of rum, until he came to the cottage which later became the Shipwright's. He banged on the door, pleading to be let in, but the occupants were too frightened or selfish to do so. The seaman collapsed from exhaustion and died of exposure on the doorstep. Ever since, it is said, he has haunted the Shipwright's Arms. The ghost is described as being of 'an old sailor, wearing a reefer jacket and peaked cap, and smelling strongly of rum and tobacco'. He has been known to appear, somewhat disconcertingly, in the bedrooms, glaring at the occupants with wide, staring eyes.

Ghost walks and even televised ghost hunts have become a popular feature at the Historic Dockyard at **Chatham** in recent years. The Historic Dockyard has seen ships built, repaired and manned from the days of the Spanish Armada through to the Falklands Crisis. It is now a prestigious visitor attraction and is often used as a film set. Visitors and members of staff have reported a great deal of paranormal activity here. A ghostly wagon, driven by a man in a long

Faversham's Guildhall dates back to the 16th century. It is haunted by a heavily pacing ghost. Shutterstock/ Paul J Martin

coat and tall hat, has been both seen and heard, and in broad daylight. A lady in grey haunts the Sail and Colours Loft and has the odd habit of poking people in the back. In the Commissioner's House a staircase is haunted by a woman who hanged herself from the top banister, and five ghostly children have been seen singly or in groups in an attic room. Children in raggedy clothing have also been seen in the quarter-mile-long Ropery building.

The superstar spook of the docks, however, is none other than Admiral Lord Nelson. The hero of Trafalgar and many other naval victories is said to stride around the Historic Dockyard with a confident air. The apparition is of a youthful Nelson, dating from the years before he lost an arm and an eye.

Two buildings in the High Street are haunted respectively by a 'Man in Green' and a young woman who is absorbed in the simple pleasure of brushing her hair. Peter Underwood states that neighbouring houses in Magpie Hall Road have long been possessed of mysterious footsteps followed by an urgent tapping as if someone wanted to be let in. On the nights when they've been heard, the noises would begin at about midnight and often continue right through till dawn. A man committed suicide in one of the properties and it was thought his troubled spirit was behind the haunting.

A number of ghosts haunt **Royal Tunbridge Wells**. In the Pantiles, the Georgian centre of the town, the phantom of a woman in grey has been seen. Some think she may be Sarah Porter, assistant to the dandy Beau Nash, who virtually ruled over the place during the Regency period. Mysterious running footsteps have been heard around the shores of Mulberry Lake in Rusthall Park. By far the strangest spook haunting Tunbridge Wells, however, is the ghostly white limousine which motors round its narrow streets. The car dates from the 1920s and is exceedingly grand, although its make is a little uncertain: it has been variously identified as a Rolls-Royce, Daimler or Bentley. As well as being white in colour and old-fashioned, the vehicle is distinctive for having darkened windows. After a little motoring, the car pulls up beside the road then 'shimmers and shakes as if it were a reflection in wind-ruffled water' (to quote Rupert Matthews) before vanishing.

Over in **Tonbridge**, the name of the Cardinal's Error pub refers to Cardinal Wolsey, who lived here for a while when the building was still a farmhouse. Wolsey's 'error' was to accept the post of Papal Legate during the reign of Henry

A youthful Horatio Nelson is one of the ghosts encountered at the Historic Dockyards at Chatham. Shutterstock/ Georgios Kollidas

VIII just as the King was contemplating his split from the Roman Catholic Church. Accused of high treason, Wolsey died on the way to his hearing in London. The spooky footsteps that are heard pacing up and down a corridor are optimistically identified as those of the over-ambitious cardinal. The visible ghost, however, is of a rather handsome woman in a large hat, who from time to time bursts into a bedroom and then throws herself out of a window.

The core of the splendid Museum and Art Gallery in **Maidstone** is an Elizabethan manor house. When England's 'spectre inspector' Andrew Green was working in the Adult Education Centre next door to the museum in the 1980s he learnt of a weird phenomenon associated with the painting of a gypsy girl in the Baxter Print Room. Many

A vintage white limousine, similar to this aptly named Rolls-Royce Wraith, drives sedately round Tunbridge Wells before suddenly vanishing.
Shutterstock/ Trybex

people had reported a 'weird feeling' around the picture, as if it emanated 'peculiar waves of some invisible force'. Equally strange but rather more chilling was the phenomenon reported from the 18th-century manor house which forms part of the Maidstone Hospital complex. In 1979 members of staff heard hysterical sobbing, apparently made by a woman, coming from one of the wards. No one was ever found to account for the distressing sound.

Heading to the coast now, and the Dreamland entertainment complex in **Margate** has had a haunted reputation since at least the 1990s. Staff members have been scared by the sounds of disembodied footsteps and an eerie whispering in an area of the fun park where a murder was committed more than a hundred years ago. The phantom of a former stallholder has also been seen strolling about the place. Margate's other well-known haunted spot is the Theatre Royal, described as 'one of the oldest surviving theatres in the UK'. It is haunted by an actor who committed suicide by jumping from one of the boxes into the orchestra pit.

Below **Ramsgate** is a series of tunnels carved out of the chalk during the Second World War. They were used as air raid shelters and then, after the war, sealed up. According to the Thanet Ghostwatch website, the tunnels 'are said to be haunted', but because they are currently inaccessible any further information on the nature of the haunting is elusive. A town centre roundabout (where the old A253, now the A299, meets the A256) is over the spot where criminals were formerly hung in chains. A weird pulsating light has been glimpsed from time to time swinging backwards and forwards above the roundabout, in the same way a corpse might swing in a high wind.

Spooky activity has been experienced in the incongruous surroundings of the Dreamland fun park on Margate's seafront. Shutterstock/ Concept Photo

Andrew Green took part in a paranormal investigation some years ago at a derelict house formerly owned by the military at Shorncliffe Camp near **Folkestone**. Then called Underhill House, it had a grim history, with no fewer than three suicides and one murder having taken place there since it was built in the 1840s. Many occupants during its period of habitation had reported creepy experiences, and on his visit Mr Green and his colleagues witnessed one odd occurrence. He and his two fellow investigators heard a tinkle of glass in a corridor behind them and turned to find a light-bulb gently rocking on the floor about ten feet away. When Mr Green picked it up, he found it was still warm despite the fact that the electricity had been cut off at Underhill House months earlier.

A woman in a white nightgown is said to haunt the fourth floor of Folkestone's luxury Clifton Hotel. The local legend is that this is the ghost of a woman who killed herself in one of the bedrooms on the break-up of a love affair. In a room on the floor below, unaccountable noises like the moving about of heavy furniture have been heard. On one occasion a night porter approaching the room to investigate the sounds felt an invisible hand grab his.

In 2011 a so-called 'groping ghost' became headline news. A **Herne Bay** grandmother complained that she was being bothered at night by an invisible intruder. The 73-year-old told the *Herne Bay Times*: 'I was lying in bed when I felt this creepy pair of hands. I kicked frantically and it went away. Next time it came I hurled the duvet on to the floor! But the ghost keeps coming back. I've tried sleeping without the duvet. But it started shaking my mattress. I even threw the mattress off the bed and bought a new one but it has made no difference.'

She continued: 'It's like an octopus. It's harassing me. I told the vicar and he said it is a lost spirit. What I want to know is, why has it got lost in my flat?' The *Herne Bay Times* called in a husband and wife team of mediums to get rid of the troublesome spook.

Herne Bay, where a very annoying ghost invaded an elderly woman's flat a few years ago. Shutterstock/ Paul J Martin

THE MOST HAUNTED VILLAGE?

For decades **Pluckley** rejoiced under the title of the Most Haunted Village in England. I say rejoiced, but over the years Pluckley's spooky status attracted not just lovers of ghost stories but also a rowdy element which would descend on the village at Halloween, making a nuisance of themselves. So much annoyance was caused that the police took to cordoning off the village on the night of 31 October and sending visitors elsewhere.

Pluckley's 'most haunted' title was awarded because at least a dozen ghosts are claimed to haunt its houses, streets and immediate surroundings. A phantom coach and horses trundles down the village's High Street in the early hours of the morning. It is occasionally seen – the coachman is said to be headless – but more often heard, as the thump of hooves and the jingling of harness. The Red Lady haunts St Nicholas's Church, usually inside but she occasionally wanders around the graveyard, too. The church is also haunted by a woman in white, believed to be a former Lady Dering, and in addition a little white dog. The two pubs are haunted and so is the Dering Arms restaurant. A Tudor lady has been seen gliding through Rose Court. Greystones, on Station Road, is haunted by a friendly monk and a little girl who died after eating ivy.

At the Pinnock Bridge there is the ghost of an old watercress seller who burnt to death when her clay pipe fell among her clothing. At the suitably named Fright Corner a highwayman was 'pinned like a butterfly' to an oak tree by the sword of an intended victim who proved more than his match, and he is doomed to suffer his grisly fate over and over again.

A White Lady may still haunt the site of her former home, Surrenden Dering, which was destroyed by fire some years ago. This may well be the same ghost which haunts the churchyard. The estate's woods were formerly haunted by a colonel who hanged himself from one of the trees, but these have now been largely cut down. Another area of woodland is known as the 'screaming woods' because of the eldritch cries heard emanating from it, but this should not be confused with the site of a former brickworks where the bloodcurdling screams of a man who fell to his death into a deep pit can still be heard.

The Dering Arms restaurant is an old hunting lodge at Pluckley. In common with many other properties in this 'most haunted village', it is said to have its ghosts.
Shutterstock/ Neil Wigmore

Elvey Farm is a medieval farmstead turned boutique hotel. It has a number of ghosts, including that of farmer Edward Brett, who shot himself in the dairy. The ghost is said to move objects around, slam doors shut and make various crashes and bangs around the house. The unpleasant smell of burning wool has also been detected here for reasons unknown.

MORE FROM THE VILLAGES

Pluckley is by no means Kent's only haunted village. One Christmas Eve, according to tradition, a highwayman held up a coach carrying an elderly man and his daughter into **Marden** along the Hawkhurst Road. He commanded them out of the vehicle, but just as the young woman had stepped onto the road, the horses bolted, and the coach leapt away. The coachman and the old gentleman were frantic at the thought of the girl being left at the mercy of the ruffian. However, by the time the horses were brought under control and they had succeeded in returning to help, they found something entirely unexpected: the highwayman lying slumped by the side of the road, dying of a stab wound. There was no sign of the girl.

Before he died, the highwayman was able to choke out an explanation. He told the astonished old man that his daughter had recognised him as the robber who had killed her brother some years previously. Vowing vengeance, she had suddenly produced a blade and stabbed him to the heart.

They found the young woman the following morning, hiding in a wood. She had gone completely out of her mind. Every Christmas Eve, for many years, the strange adventure was replayed in ghostly form at the spot where it had occurred.

The similarly named village of **Smarden** has a haunted pub, The Chequers. Shortly after the Napoleonic Wars came to an end, an army officer called at this 14th-century coaching inn. He was returning home with a considerable sum of money accrued during his years of service. The young barmaid immediately set her sights on him and charmed him into staying the night. She was not nearly as charming as she had seemed, however. After the soldier had fallen asleep, she stealthily began to make off with his gold.

Smarden is haunted by a soldier who was murdered for the money he had saved during the wars with Napoleon. Shutterstock/ Andrew Fletcher

Unfortunately, she wasn't stealthy enough and he woke up. The girl silenced him with a knife, and fled with the booty. The ghost of the murdered soldier still makes his presence known by pacing around Room 6, where the tragedy happened, and also in the kitchen, where he delights in moving or hiding utensils and occasionally introducing utensils which no one has seen before.

The echo of a terrible accident from a past age is said to still be played out in **Grafty Green**. Marc Alexander recounts the story in his *Phantom Britain*: 'In the old coaching days, a coach-and-four departed from the village bound for Lenham late at night. After the driver had whipped up his horses they took fright for some unknown reason and bolted. When the swaying vehicle reached the bend by the local church, the panic stricken animals charged to the right instead of taking the left fork of the road. As a result they galloped up a driveway into the grounds of the old rectory and crashed into a tree. The impact killed the horses immediately and smashed the coach to pieces. The driver was catapulted from his seat with such force that he was decapitated on the branch of a tree.'

Mr Alexander continues that villagers passing by the rectory after dark would sometimes be horrified by the sound of frantic hooves, the rattle and creak of the coach followed by the sounds of a terrible smash and the screams of both horses and passengers.

Ghostly hoofbeats heard at St Mary's Church, **Kemsing**, are believed to belong to the horse of one of the men who assassinated Thomas Becket in Canterbury Cathedral in 1170. A local tradition has it the guilt-ridden knight rode to the ancient church to seek absolution. In Watery Lane, a phantom Cavalier has been seen. His reason for haunting is also guilt. He belonged to a party of Royalists who had gathered to discuss their next move during the English Civil War. One of them spotted a youngster named William hanging about on the other side of a hedge. Taking the unfortunate William for a spy, they promptly hanged him from a nearby tree. The ghostly Cavalier haunts the spot where the cruel deed was carried out, eternally regretting it.

The Wild Rider is the name given to the spectral horseman of **Hollingbourne**. He charges through the village on a

Hollingbourne is one of several horsey haunts in Kent. Here the so-called Wild Rider gallops through the village at breakneck speed. Shutterstock/ Jo Ann Snover

black stallion at a reckless speed, urging his mount on with savage cuts of his crop. When horse and rider reach the gates of Hollingbourne House, they vanish. The horseman is thought to be a former owner of Hollingbourne House who foolishly tried to leap the gates and died as a result. The ghost haunting the church at Hollingbourne is a much more peaceful presence. She is Lady Grace Gethin, a remarkably pious person who suddenly went into a trance during a church service and experienced a vision lasting two hours of 'heavenly glory … triumphing over death'. She died the very next day, though (in 1697).

Yet another 'horsey' ghost haunts **Rainham**. This is a black coach which materialises outside the church at midnight on nights when the moon is full. The coach is pulled by headless black horses and the coachman is headless, too. A black-clad figure emerges from the graveyard and climbs into the coach, where he removes his own head. Then the coachman whips up the horses and the spectral coach lurches away from the churchyard gate and away through the narrow lanes, sparks flying from its wheels, until it reaches Bloors Place, a Tudor manor house.

In the late 17th century Bloors Place was the home of Christopher Bloor, a man of riotous living and womanising habits. One night Bloor was found dead on the road outside the house. Rumour had it he had been done in by the father of one of his many wronged women. There was no evidence of violence, however, which led to a stranger rumour: that the Devil had simply claimed his soul. It is his spirit that is seen to enter the funereal coach, which then drives him to the scene of his earthly debauches.

Another unusual haunting is recounted by Peter Underwood in his *Gazetteer of British Ghosts* as taking place at **Saltwood**, near Hythe. This ghost is described as 'a man in a red cloak carrying a lantern'. This mysterious figure has appeared in various places around the village, in neighbouring roads, woods and fields. Sometimes only the light of the lantern is seen, or a 'ball of fire' which transforms into the cloaked figure.

The rectory at **Southfleet**, near Gravesend, is haunted by 'a female figure wearing a brown nun-like habit'. In 1874 the Bishop of Rochester visited the rectory to exorcise the ghost. He doesn't seem to have been too successful, however. Peter Underwood gathered data on the apparition from four independent eye-witnesses, all post-dating the Bishop's visit. It was seen by the incumbent resident between 1891 and 1898, then on a number of occasions during the 1910s and 1920s (a servant stated that the figure seemed to be searching for something), and in February 1942 the Revd Falloon saw it in broad daylight during his time at the rectory. He told Mr Underwood she was 'about four feet seven inches in height; dumpy in shape and wearing a brown serge overall dress, with a brown tippet reaching to the elbows and a close-fitting brown serge cap'. Local legend has it this unfortunate little woman was walled up alive in the cellars after being found 'in company' with a monk (the rectory stands on the site of a medieval friary).

One of the strangest and most disturbing Kent spectres was encountered by writer Joan Forman. In her *Haunted East Anglia*, Ms Forman explains that in the 1950s she was working in the village school in **Goudhurst**. During the first few days of the summer holidays, she was sleeping alone in an old part of the school. One night she awoke to find a weird creature crouching in her room. It was the size of a corgi but had large, lemur-like eyes that seemed to emit a glow. It turned its eyes to her.

'I think it was the most revolting gaze I ever had to endure,' she writes, 'for what emanated from that thing was an atmosphere of extreme malevolence and obscenity. With all its exudation of evil it was at the same time mocking.' The thing held her in its thrall until the first rays of dawn were upon it, when it suddenly vanished.

A tranquil scene in Goudhurst, hardly the place one would expect to encounter an 'atmosphere of extreme malevolence' as writer Joan Forman did.
Shutterstock/ Andrew Fletcher

HISTORIC HAUNTED HOUSES

Dean Manor, a timber-framed house at Meopham dating back to the early 15th century, became the centre of a celebrated ghost hunt in 1936. The famous (or infamous depending on your point of view) paranormal researcher Harry Price broadcast live on BBC Radio as he carried out his investigation at Dean Manor. Price had been called in by the then owner, a Mr Varley, who had seen the ghost of a servant girl several times during the first few months of his residency. He was so afraid of the ghost that on one occasion he lobbed a poker at it.

Mr Varley and his family would be sitting in the lounge when the apparition, bold as you like, would open the door and walk in. Then the spooky servant would stand stock still as if waiting for orders. In addition to this unwelcome presence, the Varleys would hear inexplicable footsteps and eerie 'mutterings' about the place, and someone or something would open up the cellar door several times a day, but only when no one was looking. Harry Price's investigation was inconclusive, although he and his team did record a dramatic fall in temperature live on air. One member of the BBC crew heard mysterious footsteps when he slept in the house after the broadcast.

Cleve Court, at Monkton, is another private residence with a phantom lady. The ghost's history is a tragic one. She was the wife of Joseph Farrer, a brute of a man who spent all his time on his own pleasure, which largely consisted of womanising and drinking to excess. Mrs Farrer remonstrated and pleaded with her husband to mend his ways but his response was to lock her up. In this way he was free to indulge himself without censure or embarrassment. He kept his wife incarcerated for years, until she finally succumbed to her despair and died. In the following years a number of people have heard the pacing of high-heeled shoes in the room where Mrs Farrer was kept a prisoner. In addition the apparition of a woman dressed in grey, with a cape and a white ribbon in her hair, has been seen about the house. She is presumed to be the ghost of Mrs Farrer but became known simply as the Grey Lady.

One of Kent's most interesting and picturesque old houses is **Ightham Mote**, near Sevenoaks. Now in the care of the National Trust, Ightham Mote is a wonderfully preserved 14th-century moated manor house. For centuries it was the home of the Selby family. In 1605 an anonymous letter was sent to Lord Monteagle warning him not to attend the Houses of Parliament on the coming 5 November. It was through this letter that the Gunpowder Plot was discovered and foiled. It is believed the author of the letter was Dame Dorothy Selby, and that she may have been done away with for writing it. In 1872 a blocked-up doorway was uncovered in one of the towers at Ightham Mote. When it was smashed through, a woman's skeleton was found huddled in a cupboard. Was it Dame Dorothy's? No one can say for sure, but ever since the bones were discovered an unaccountable chill has been felt in that part of the house. Even an exorcism by a bishop failed to remove the unearthly chill. The female phantom glimpsed from time to time around Ightham Mote is also presumed to be Dame Dorothy.

The magnificent medieval manor house of Ightham Mote literally had a skeleton in a cupboard. Shutterstock/ Mark Bridger

A creepy coldness is a feature of another Kent haunting, this time at **Wrotham House** in the village of Wrotham. The sensation occurs in one of the rooms, where a man murdered his brother in his bed and then threw his body out of the window. Even more chilling than the atmospheric chilliness is the sinister chuckle which is heard in the room: an echo of the killer's mirthless laugh after the deed was done. The story of the haunting first appeared in *The Ghost Book* of Lord Halifax, published in 1936. In it he reprinted a letter from a Mrs Brooke, dated April 1883, in which she outlined her own experiences and those of her husband while staying in the house.

The nurse looking after Mrs Brooke's infant son, while Mrs Brooke was chatting with her hostess until about one o'clock in the morning, told her that 'someone had been playing practical jokes on her'. She said the door to the bedroom opened, someone laughed, then it was closed again. This happened a number of times. The nurse locked the door but the mysterious intruder was still able to open it. Mrs Brooke had noticed the 'vault-like coldness' of the room for herself. The next morning her hostess admitted that the room was haunted and told her the story behind it.

The following night it was Mrs Brooke's turn to experience the ghost. She felt the temperature plummet and heard stealthy footsteps approaching the door. Someone, or something, fumbled with the door. Then 'The figure of a man, clothed in a grey suit trimmed with silver and wearing a cocked hat, walked in and stood by the side of the bed furthest from me, with his face turned away from the window. I lay in mortal terror watching him, but he turned, still with his back to me, went out of the door uttering a horrid little laugh, and walked some paces down the passage, returning again and again.'

On the third night, the nurse slept on the sofa in the room with her mistress and the ghostly visitation was repeated. Despite her hostess's assurances that the ghost only visited three times and she wouldn't see him again, Mrs Brooke decided enough was enough and went home. The real mystery to me is why the resident family didn't simply put Mrs Brooke in a different room!

When Sir Harold Nicolson and the novelist Vita Sackville-West bought **Sissinghurst Castle**, near Cranbrook, in 1930 they found themselves with a dilapidated Elizabethan

Sissinghurst's Elizabethan gatehouse is a striking feature of its celebrated gardens. The gardens are haunted. © *National Trust*

mansion, hardly deserving the title of 'castle'. They transformed the place into a luxurious home and the grounds into world-famous gardens still visited by thousands every year (Sissinghurst is now a National Trust property). The apparition of a tall, thin figure wearing a black cloak wanders the grounds. Because he tends to be seen near the Priest's House he is referred to as 'the Priest', but his identity is in truth a mystery.

Knole House, near Sevenoaks, is an even grander manor house, surrounded by a vast wooded estate. The sorrowing shade of a finely dressed woman has been seen in the grounds, making her melancholy way down an avenue of hornbeams called the Duchess Walk. Some believe her to be a former Duchess of Dorset after whom the avenue is named; others that she is the ghost of a member of the resident Sackville family who found herself in an unhappy marriage.

At least two ghosts have been reported from the grounds of Knole House, a vast Elizabethan–Stuart property near Sevenoaks.
Shutterstock/ Standa Riha

Vita Sackville-West, who was born at Knole House, referred in one of her writings to a cottage in the park which had a 'sinister atmosphere'. This may be the same one that was reported as haunted some years ago. It was the home of a park warden and his family. The warden's wife came in from the garden and was alarmed to see a strange man approaching the room where her young child was sleeping. She challenged the intruder, only to see him vanish before her eyes. The ghost was never seen so clearly again but a vague, human-shaped form was glimpsed on the stairs from time to time.

Knole House and its park are now managed by the National Trust. Only a few miles from Ightham Mote, these two splendid old haunted houses can easily be visited on the same day.

Another grand place to visit is **Penshurst Place**, near Tonbridge. Described as 'the grandest and most perfectly preserved fortified manor house in England', Penshurst Place boasts an eleven-acre garden among its attractions. It was the birthplace of Sir Philip Sidney, Elizabethan poet, soldier and courtier, who earned the flattering nickname of 'the perfection of men'. His elegant figure, complete with ruff, doublet and hose, is said to still be seen around Penshurst.

Chiddingstone Castle, Edenbridge, started life as a Tudor manor house but its current castellated appearance dates from a major reconstruction in the early 19th century. Chiddingstone is a splendid show home famous for its collections of rare and beautiful artefacts collected from around the world by a former antiquarian owner. Its grounds are haunted by a defunct lady of the house, wearing a riding habit and tricorn hat, who canters about on an equally phantom horse.

Combe Bank, at Sundridge, is a charming Palladian-style 18th-century mansion based on one of Rome's most beautiful houses, the Villa Doria. It is now a private girls' school. Combe Bank's present peaceful existence belies a bloody past. In 1760 the wife of the fourth Earl Ferrers brought a petition of separation against him because of his constant ill-treatment of her. One of his stewards gave evidence in support of Lady Ferrers's claim. The Earl was so angry that he shot the man dead. Somewhat to his surprise, this cruel and arrogant man found himself tried and convicted of murder. He seemed to think he could do whatever he liked with his servants, even kill them. Lord Ferrers asked to be executed on Tower Hill but to his chagrin he wasn't considered exalted enough and instead he was dragged to 'Tyburn Tree', the public scaffold in London.

'I think it hard that I must die at the place appointed for the execution of common felons,' sniffed this extraordinary man. On observing the crowds gathered to watch him swing, he said: 'I suppose they never saw a lord hanged and will never see another.'

The only concession given to his lordly status was that he was hanged with a silken rope rather than one made of hemp. However, it is not Lord Ferrers who haunts Combe Bank but his unfortunate wife. One can only imagine the sort of life she led during her marriage to her murderous and insufferable first husband, and it seems an even greater tragedy that she should have died anything but peacefully. In 1807 Lady Ferrers was burnt to death in a fire in one of the towers. It is thought she dozed off and fell into the fireplace in her dressing room. After the blaze had burnt itself out, all that was found of the poor woman was one thumb, and this was interred with all due ceremony at Sundridge church.

For years after, it was said, the spectral form of this unlucky woman would be seen walking round the park at Combe Bank, looking for her missing thumb. Fortunately for the

Combe Bank, sketched by Charles Harper for his 1907 book on Haunted Houses.

young ladies now attending Combe Bank School, the phantom Lady Ferrers has not been encountered for many years.

A LOST HAUNTED HOUSE

Great Bayhall Manor House is now, alas, no longer with us. For years it was the most famously haunted house in Kent. Situated near Pembury, Great Bayhall was already in a state of disrepair when it was visited by Charles Harper in the early 1900s while he was researching his seminal work on *Haunted Houses*. Harper quotes the following newspaper account of the ghostly goings-on reported at the abandoned mansion in the 1890s:

'The old manor, with its moss-grown roof, its broken doors and windows and its old moat, can be traced back to the reign of King John. For several weeks past persons residing in the immediate neighbourhood have been startled by unearthly noises and groans, and many of the villagers have been heard to declare that they have seen ghostly figures walking about. Such has been the sensation caused in Tunbridge Wells, that a number of well-known gentlemen have visited the house and heard what they believe to be "true spirit noises". The investigators were armed with heavy sticks, and for upwards of an hour awaited the first sound which was to signal the presence of the ghosts.'

When this finally came, even the heavy sticks were not enough to give the 'investigators' sufficient courage to face

down the alleged ghosts: 'According to the story told by one
of them, they were straining eye and ear when suddenly a
rumbling noise like the dragging of some heavy body across

*Lonely and abandoned Great Bayhall Manor House sketched by Charles
Harper in the early 1900s.*

the floor broke the silence of the night. One or two of the explorers were paralysed with fear, but the rest were sufficiently courageous to enter the house. In the cellar below there was a succession of thuds, followed by groans and the result was that the party beat a hasty retreat. Visits have been paid by other parties, who have reported the groans as "terrible".'

All this spooky activity was blamed on the restless spirit of one Anne West, who is buried in a tomb in Pembury churchyard. Anne had suffered the terrifying ordeal of having been nearly buried alive during an illness. To ensure nothing similar could happen again, she stipulated a number of safeguards for her genuine demise (which eventually took place in 1803). She is supposed to have left her fortune to a servant on the condition that he daily place bread and water on her coffin for twelve months after her interment. A more favoured local tradition was that she stipulated that she should be placed in her vault in a coffin without a lid and that ventilation be provided.

For years, youngsters would dare each other to push items through a ventilation hole in the brickwork, believing that they would fall into Anne's open coffin. In fact, the tomb below is sealed and the hole leads to nothing more than a small air-chamber. Charles Harper noticed that the custom was still much in evidence on his own visit. He wrote: 'There are many evidences, in the shape of half-burnt matches around the grille, and in the stones half pushed through, and the plaster picked out of the church walls, that the story is well known and the place plentifully visited.'

Anne West was the last person to reside at Great Bayhall Manor House and this fact, combined with her supposedly eccentric burial, seems to have been enough for popular imagination to have connected her to the ghostly goings-on

Pembury Church, where a tomb can be found which at one time had a weird reputation among the local populace.

at her former home. Interest in the ghost was revived in the late 1950s by a newspaper article and once again the landowner found himself plagued with curious trespassers. The manor house was by then entirely ruinous and the nuisance caused by the sightseers was enough to win for him an order to tear it down. Nothing now remains above ground of Great Bayhall Manor House, but Anne West's tomb in Pembury churchyard can still be visited.

THE MYSTERIOUS CHILDREN

In the Eden Valley, on a minor road between Leigh and Hildenborough, there stands venerable **Ramhurst Manor**. Ramhurst dates back to the 16th century but was largely remodelled in the 18th century. During the latter period it was the home of a family who, if the story is true, continued to linger on in the house long after their death.

In an early work on ghost-lore, *Footfalls on the Boundary of Another World* by Robert Dale Owen, we learn of an extraordinary haunting at Ramhurst. In 1857, a family Owen only identifies by the initial 'R' moved into the old manor house. They found it to be haunted by strange noises: taps, thumps, whispered voices and stealthy footsteps. The cook heard the swishing of a silk dress pass her in an empty corridor. Terrifying screams echoed through the house at three o'clock in the morning but no one was found to account for them.

While 'Mr R' was away serving in India, 'Mrs R' invited an old friend, a 'Miss S', to stay. Miss S had long considered herself to be psychic and had seen a number of apparitions over the years. Miss S was collected from the railway station and as the open carriage approached Ramhurst Manor, she saw an elderly couple dressed in the fashions of the 18th century standing outside the front door. So as not to alarm Mrs R, she said nothing about her vision. Over the next few days, however, Miss S saw the same couple on a number of occasions, always in daylight and surrounded by a 'grey haze'. Unfazed, the psychic lady succeeded in communicating with the ghostly couple. They told her their name was 'Children', the man adding that his first name was Richard and that he had died in 1753.

Miss S now confided in her friend as to what she had seen. Shortly afterwards, Mrs R also saw the ghosts, standing in a doorway. Above the woman's head she saw, outlined in luminous letters, the words 'Dame Children'. She also received an imperfect impression or communication from the woman that 'her hopes and fears having been entirely of this earth, she was "earth-bound"'. Mrs R's brother was calling for her at this moment, and she rushed through where the phantoms were standing to join him. Miss S was also present. 'Oh, my dear,' exclaimed Mrs R, 'I've walked through Mrs Children!'

Neither the 'R' family nor the near neighbours were aware of a family called Children ever having lived in Ramhurst Manor. It had indeed gone through several hands before Mr and Mrs R moved in. At this point, Robert Dale Owen became involved. His historical research revealed that a

Richard Children had indeed lived at Ramhurst Manor and had died there in 1753, aged 83 years. Although the house had belonged to the Children family for many years, and remained in the family's possession until 1816, Richard was the only member of the family to be in residence there.

Writing in 1907, Charles Harper records: 'The tale is still current in the neighbourhood that the house will be haunted until the property comes back into the Children family; but not for many years past has anyone been disturbed by ghostly sights and sounds.'

Charles Harper's sketch of Ramhurst Manor house where, in the 1850s, a haunting was apparently confirmed by historical research.

KENT
Ghost Stories

HAUNTED CASTLES AND NOBLE RUINS

Dover, Rochester and Canterbury. Ancient and noble castles and all of them haunted. They are not the only haunted castles in Kent, however. Indeed Kent is blessed with some exceptionally beautiful castles, well preserved or surviving as atmospheric ruins. In addition, the remains of medieval monastic houses can be found throughout the county. Many of these remnants of the past are 'ghosted', to use an old-fashioned term.

Leeds Castle, between Maidstone and Ashford, is an iconic place. The fortified manor house, surrounded by a stone wall, rises out of a wide moat from a green island like something from a medieval fable. A castle was built here in the 12th century and later became a favourite home of Edward I and then the residence of Henry VIII's first queen, Catherine of Aragon. It was largely remodelled in the early 19th century, however. Leeds Castle and its grounds are open to the public.

In the 15th century the Duchess of Gloucester was imprisoned here on charges of practising sorcery. If she hadn't been an aunt of King Henry VI she would almost certainly have been executed. Legend has it that the Duchess failed to give up her witchy ways, for soon after she was incarcerated at Leeds Castle a huge black dog began to be seen about the countryside. No one knew where it had come from, but those who saw it felt there was something uncanny about it. Some thought it was the Duchess's familiar spirit, others that it was the sorceress herself in canine form.

61

The splendid moated fortress of Leeds Castle was formerly used as a gaol for a notorious royal witch. Shutterstock/ MARKABOND

The Black Dog of Leeds is now said to haunt the castle and its environs. To see it is thought to bring misfortune. However, for one 19th-century witness it was an exceedingly lucky sighting. She was sitting on a bench up against the castle walls when a huge black hound loped past. Curious about the animal, she rose to follow it – just as a huge lump of masonry fell from the wall and crushed the bench she had been sitting on. The ghost of the wicked Duchess of Gloucester – in human form – has also been seen about the place.

As mentioned above, Leeds Castle is a former home of King Henry VIII's first wife. His second wife, the ill-fated Anne Boleyn, grew up at the equally splendid **Hever Castle** (which later passed to Henry's fourth wife, Anne of Cleves). Hever, near Edenbridge, is a 13th-century castle with Tudor additions and a glorious Italianate garden created by a much later occupant, William Waldorf Astor. It is another popular visitor attraction. Anne Boleyn lived here until she was fifteen. Her marriage to Henry VIII was far from a happy one, as everyone knows. She gave him one child, the future Elizabeth I, but after that a stillborn boy and no future male heir. Henry had already met Jane Seymour by this time and a – probably – trumped-up charge of adultery was made against Anne and five supposed lovers. All six were executed.

Shortly after Anne was put to death, her apparition began to be seen about Hever Castle. It was said her ghost was brought home in a spectral carriage which glided over the river and deposited her at the front door. Now she wanders the castle and gardens, a sweet smile upon her face, as if grateful to be back in the place where she enjoyed her happier and more innocent childhood years.

Lympne Castle, near Hythe, is another wonderfully archaic building, now a rather grand home which is also run as a unique setting for weddings and corporate events. It is full of history. A Roman fortress formerly stood on the site. The Saxons then built their own fort here but had it forcibly taken off them by marauding Danes. This wooden fort was replaced by a stone castle after the Norman Conquest and Thomas Becket lived here for a while. During the Tudor period the castle was converted into a more comfortable manor house. Thanks to its commanding views of the sea, Lympne Castle has also been used as an observation post, by smugglers during the 18th century and by the armed forces during the Second World War.

Lympne Castle's ghosts are among the most ancient in Kent. A Roman legionary haunts the eastern tower. He can be heard tramping up it but not returning because he tripped and fell to his death after reaching the top. Also of some antiquity are the ghosts of six Saxon men who got trapped in the castle and were hunted down and killed by Norman soldiers shortly after the Conquest.

Henry VIII's second wife, Anne Boleyn, haunts her childhood home, Hever Castle.
Shutterstock/Jo Tunney

Scotney Old Castle – another beautiful moated fortress – has had if anything a riper history than Lympne. In 1259 its owner, Walter de Scotney, poisoned the Earl of Gloucester and a party of noblemen who were dining with the Bishop of Winchester. He didn't do a very good job: several people died but the Earl was not one of them. Walter de Scotney was hanged and his estates passed to the Darrell family. During the persecution of the Catholics during the 16th century, the family priest made a bolt for it during a search of the castle and swam his way to freedom across the moat. A century or so later another member of the Darrell family faked his own death to avoid paying his debts and even had the cheek to join the mourners at his funeral. Later Darrells became smugglers and at one point were besieged by excise men.

It is from this period that the ghost of the Old Castle dates. During a scrap with revenue officers, a Darrell killed one of them. In order to cover up the crime, he threw the body into the moat. The deed was not allowed to be forgotten, however. For some years after the deed, the ghost of the murdered man would emerge from the moat and then bang on the front door, demanding his killer be brought to justice.

Scotney Castle (as opposed to the Old Castle) is a lovely stately home. The house, gardens and the ruin of the Old Castle nearby are all in the care of the National Trust and are situated near Lamberhurst.

Right on the Sussex border not far from Scotney Castle can be found the remains of **Bayham Old Abbey**. Dating mainly from the 13th century, the ruins were slightly modified to make them more picturesque by the landscape gardener Humphry Repton. This took place in the late 18th century when they became a prominent feature in the grounds of Bayham Abbey manor house. The ruins are now in the care of English Heritage. The ghosts of this ancient monastic building are what you might expect: phantom monks. They process in pairs up the choir to what remains of

The ruins of Old Bayham Abbey are haunted by those who used to live and pray here. © English Heritage

the high altar. In addition, the sound of monks' chanting has been heard emanating from the ruins and the aroma of incense has also been detected from time to time.

Of a similar age to Bayham Old Abbey, **Old Soar Manor House** at Plaxtol is a rare survival of 13th-century domestic architecture. Only a few rooms of the manor house survive but they are complete. Inexplicable footsteps and sudden cold spots have been experienced at Old Soar Manor House and the apparition of a priest in a black cloak has also been seen. This may be the same priest who, according to the unpleasant tale attached to the house, seduced a maid-servant and left her with child. The girl hanged herself in her shame and despair. Old Soar Manor House is also in the care of English Heritage.

The ghost of a former servant girl has also been seen about **Allington Castle**, north of Maidstone. The castle was in a ruinous state by the end of the 19th century but was then restored and is now a private home. The maid-servant gave birth to an illegitimate child, which she then drowned in the moat. The girl was hanged for the crime.

The mighty Norman keep of **Chilham Castle** still stands in the grounds of the splendid Jacobean manor house that now bears its name. Despite being constructed in the 12th century, the keep is no ruin but is still inhabited. Both are private homes, however, and not open to the public. A phantom woman wearing 'a magnificent gown' haunts the keep. Strange sounds, like the dragging about of heavy furniture, have been heard in an upper room. When Andrew Green visited the keep in 1975 he was lucky enough to hear the sounds for himself but was unable to find an explanation for them.

The low walls of **Richborough Roman Fort**, near Sandwich, are patrolled by ghostly Roman legionaries. It was at Richborough that Roman forces started their invasion of Britain in AD 43 and here too that the Emperor Claudius arrived to celebrate the conquest he took no active part in (a huge triumphal arch formerly stood here). Richborough was one of the most important of the so-called Saxon Shore defences, occupied by the Romans for five centuries. The ghostly Romans presumably belonged to one of the many garrisons stationed here during that long period. Normally just the sound of the tramping of their boots is heard, but occasionally the soldiers themselves have been seen, too. They look as if they are 'marching out of a mist'.

The distinctive landmark of **Reculver Towers**, five miles
east of Herne Bay, stand on the site of another Roman fort
guarding the Saxon Shore. Little remains above ground of
the fort, and the Saxon monastery that replaced it has also all
but vanished. The Towers belong to the ruined Monastery
Church of St Mary, built by the Normans. For years mariners
used the 'Twin Sisters', as they called the Towers, to help
guide them into safe harbour. Ghostly monks have been
glimpsed from time to time among the ruins. The eerie
crying of a child has also been reported, but this may be in
response to the macabre discovery of the skeletons of three
babies buried in the Roman foundations. Some think they
may be 'foundation deposits', possible sacrifices to assure the
success of the fortress.

*The Reculver Towers are the most distinctive features of an ancient site with
a spooky reputation. © English Heritage*

GHOSTS ON THE ROADS

One of the best-known ghosts from Kent is the Phantom Hitch-Hiker of **Blue Bell Hill**. Blue Bell Hill is a steep stretch of road between Maidstone and Chatham. In their weighty compendium of British folklore, *The Lore of the Land*, Jacqueline Simpson and the late Jennifer Westwood outline the history of this classic spook. The story starts in September 1968 with an article by local man Tom Harber in *The (Maidstone) Gazette*. Mr Harber told the newspaper that 'the apparition of an unknown girl is said to have repeatedly hitched a lift by the Lower Bell pub at the foot of the hill to go into the centre of Maidstone, where she vanished from the still-moving car'.

Later the ghost girl was linked to a road accident on the night of 19 November 1965, in which three young women travelling in the same car were killed. One of the women was to be married the following day; another was to have been a bridesmaid. Tom Harber, in the 1970s, told another researcher that he'd met a man who had picked up the phantom hitch-hiker in 1966. The girl had chatted to him excitedly about her forthcoming wedding before suddenly disappearing as he was driving her to Maidstone.

By this time the story had become local legend. To confuse matters, however, some reports state that it is the bridesmaid, not the bride, who haunts the road and that occasionally she thumbs a lift in the direction of Chatham rather than Maidstone. Added to this are the reports of a much younger girl, a mere child, who steps out into the road at the same spot and is apparently run over. One motorist who suffered this horrifying experience covered the girl's body with a travel rug and then rushed to inform the police. When the

The phenomenon of the Phantom Hitch-Hiker, a young woman (usually) who hitches a lift and then vanishes while being driven to her destination, is known all over the western world. The most famous example in the UK is the one encountered at Blue Bell Hill in Kent.
Shutterstock/Alesandar Mijatovic

police returned with him, they found the rug but no girl. Now the ghostly bride (or bridesmaid) and the equally otherworldly child have blended into one: today it is said the phantom hitch-hiker of Blue Bell Hill will alarm motorists either by asking for a lift and then vanishing or by stepping into the path of oncoming cars.

A not dissimilar experience to the one had by drivers on Blue Bell Hill has also occurred on **Ide Hill**, south of Brasted. Andrew Green, in his *Haunted Kent Today*, recounts how a woman was driving up Ide Hill when her car apparently struck a young man in motorcycle leathers. The lad was nowhere to be seen when the driver shakily got out of her car. The police later informed her that she was not the only person to have seen the ghost, which was apparently that of a youth who was run down by a speeding car after he had crashed his bike.

According to *Haunted Shepway* by Paul Harris, a driver had a fright one night on the A529 just outside **Brookland**. The road passes through Romney Marsh and in this damp, low-lying area ground fogs are common. The motorist was making careful progress down the foggy road, but even so barely had time to slam on the brakes when a man suddenly emerged out of the mists and stood imperiously in front of him, his hand raised. The car went straight through the figure. There was no impact and no body was found on the road. After calming down, the driver recollected that the man's dress sense was decidedly unorthodox. He had been wearing a costume of the Elizabethan period and sporting a sharp-pointed beard. Clearly this was no human jaywalker he had encountered, but a ghost. Another driver had a similar fright on **Silver Hill** at Tenterden. She drove through the transparent figure of a man apparently dating from the 1950s, wearing skin-tight trousers and a short jacket.

A phantom coach pulled by two horses has been seen on **Elchin Hill**, near Elmsted. The hairpin bend on the hill has a reputation for unexpected breakdowns and accidents, and even a suicide. In addition to the coach, the ghosts of horsemen wearing tricorn hats have also been seen here.

A nun haunts Pennis Lane at **Fawkham Green**. The unfortunate woman was set upon by a gang of ruffians during the 1500s. Their cruel mobbing of her became increasingly violent until it became sexual assault. Two members of the local gentry heard the nun's cries for help and they rode down the thugs, who fled in panic. The rescuers then took the now unconscious and battered woman to nearby Pennis Farm, but there she died. From time to time the nun is seen at dusk in Pennis Lane, gliding in a traditionally ghostly way.

At **East Malling** a gentleman of the Victorian era has been seen strolling along the New Road towards St James's Church. The ghosts encountered on the old Watling Street at **Bridge** are from a considerably more ancient time. They are Celtic warriors marching to the place where, in AD 45, the Romans constructed the first bridge over the River Stour (the current bridge is more recent, of course). A chariot drawn by two horses and carrying a spear-bearing Ancient Briton has been seen flying down the hill, disappearing into thin air near the bridge. Tradition has it a battle was fought at Bridge between invading Roman legionaries and an army of Celts.

We have already met with a spectral limousine that makes its stately way round Tunbridge Wells. Much more dramatic – and famous – is the ghostly roadster that is said to roar its way through the village of **Patrixbourne**. This is the original Chitty Bang Bang, a racing car built in 1920 and fitted with a Zeppelin engine so mighty that the car regularly topped 100mph and won race after race.

The name of the car was borrowed by Ian Fleming for his children's book, *Chitty-Chitty-Bang-Bang*, later made into a popular film. The original car was built by Count Louis Zborowski, who lived at Higham House in Patrixbourne. Zborowski raced Chitty Bang Bang himself but in 1924 he was killed trying out a different car during a Grand Prix in Italy. Chitty Bang Bang was eventually broken up for scrap. In the years following Count Zborowski's death, he was seen again, sitting at the wheel of an equally ghostly Chitty Bang Bang and racing up the old A2 to Higham House.

SPECTRES OF THE SEA

Perhaps the most romantic inhabitants of the ghost world are the phantom ships said to ply the ocean waves long after their originals have sunk beneath the depths. The name of the *Flying Dutchman* is familiar to all but the *Northumberland* and the *Lady Lovibond* are almost as famous.

Both of these spectral ships have been encountered off the **Goodwin Sands**, a ten-mile-long sand bank in the English Channel, near Deal. The *Lady Lovibond* is said to be seen every fifty years on the anniversary of the day it sunk with all hands, 13 February 1748. The particularly tragic thing about the shipwreck is that it took place while a wedding feast was being held aboard. As Christina Hole explains in her *Haunted England*: 'Tradition has it that the steersman, a man named Rivers, had wanted to marry the bride himself, and in revenge he steered the ship on the Sands. All were drowned, and the tragic scene has repeated itself on every fiftieth anniversary since then.'

The spectral shipwreck was seen by the crews of two different ships fifty years later and there were other witnesses in 1848, 1898 and 1948. In the last of these cases, the man who made the sighting, a Captain Bull Prestwick, said the vessel was giving off a weird, greenish glow. There were no reported sightings in 1998. Will it reappear in 2048?

Even more dramatic than the *Lady Lovibond* is the apparition of the *Northumberland*. The sighting was recorded in the log of the captain of an East India Company clipper, inward bound for London: 'November 28, 1753: At ten of the clock of this day, while riding out bad weather off Goodwins, awaiting better conditions to continue our passage, an armed frigate came driving down on my ship, her masts gone, her decks and hull in fearful shape. It seemed to us all there could be no avoiding her coming athwart our anchor-chains with dire results, and I was about to order my first officer to slip our anchors when we made out the frigate for what she was.

'Her name became clear for all to read; it was *Northumberland*, and as she came on, sweeping down on my ship, we saw men running in panic about her main deck. She appeared to be unmanageable. We watched in horror, for the wind was not strong enough to place any ship in such condition, and then it pleased Almighty God the phantom, for such it surely was, steered contrary to our mounting anxieties to windward and so drove on clear of us, but no more than two ships' lengths to our leeward, and so disappeared in what seemed a dark haze.

'It was a spectacle far too terrible to dwell upon, to see this ghost of what was once a fine warship going to her doom a second time. We saw a little steady trickle of men leaping into the sea, one after another, but their bodies made no splash as they struck the waters. The cries of her spectral crew, the firing of her guns every half minute for assistance, filled us all with dread and terror that my men, as I, were nigh dead with the horror of it all.'

Fifty years earlier, on 26 November 1703, no fewer than thirteen Royal Navy warships had been lost in a typhoon that became known as 'the Great Storm'; four of them were sunk off Goodwin Sands, including the *Northumberland*. This fact was presumably known to the East India ship's captain. Of more than twelve hundred crew manning those four ships, there were only two survivors, seamen of the frigate *Mary*. In a weird twist, the survivors told how, as the *Mary* was driven crashing onto the Goodwins, 'a great warship of Drake's day, her sails tattered, burning from fore to aft and her guns firing, served by demented seamen, bore down on us, sailed right through our ship and finally disappeared before our eyes into the depth of the Sands'.

The Goodwin Sands have proved treacher-ous for hundreds of years, and if these old yarns are to be believed they are still haunted by the shades of ships that have met their doom here throughout our maritime history.

*A number of spectral ships have been seen by
experienced sailors off the Goodwin Sands, near Deal*

MRS VEAL PAYS A VISIT

One of the oldest and most interesting ghost stories set in Kent involves two best friends, a Mrs Veal and a Mrs Bargrave. The two women originally lived near to each other in Dover. Both had suffered misfortune during their lives and would regularly get together to sympathise with each other and put the world to rights. Mrs Veal would often offer her friend words of loyalty and companionship such as: 'Mrs Bargrave, you are not only the best but the only friend I have in the world, and no circumstances of life shall ever dissolve our friendship.'

Mrs Veal used to keep house for her brother. When he received an important promotion at the Custom House in Dover, she found herself moving in a different circle and the two women began to see less of each other. The separation became more enforced when Mrs Bargrave moved into a little house in Canterbury. By 1705 a couple of years had passed since the friends had last seen each other. On the morning of 8 September, Mrs Bargrave was sitting alone in her front room in Canterbury, feeling rather depressed and trying to distract herself from her gloomy thoughts with a little sewing. As the clock struck noon, there came a knock at the door. Mrs Bargrave hurried to answer it and found on the doorstep her old friend, Mrs Veal.

'Madam, I am surprised to see you; you have been so long a stranger,' said Mrs Bargrave. Then she told Mrs Veal how glad she was to see her, and leant forward to give her a kiss of welcome. But Mrs Veal evaded the kiss.

'I am not very well,' she said. She followed Mrs Bargrave inside and told her she was preparing to go on a long journey and had wanted to see her friend in Canterbury before she left. Mrs Bargrave was surprised Mrs Veal had travelled without her brother – in those days women tended not to travel alone. Mrs Veal replied: 'I gave my brother the slip and came away because I had so great a desire to see you before I took my journey.'

'My dear friend,' continued Mrs Veal, 'I am come to renew our old friendship again and to beg your pardon for my breach of it, and if you can forgive me you are the best of women. What did you think of me?'

'I thought you were like the rest of the world,' said Mrs Bargrave, 'and that prosperity had made you forget yourself and me. I can easily forgive it.'

Then the two women enjoyed a long conversation about their former friendship and what they had meant to each other in more difficult times. Their talk subsequently took an even more earnest direction. They talked about life after death and about the importance of friendship. Suddenly Mrs Veal grabbed her companion's knee.

'Dear Mrs Bargrave,' she said, 'if the eyes of our faith were as open as the eyes of our body, we should see numbers of angels about us for our guard. The notions we have of Heaven now are nothing like what it is. Therefore be comforted under your afflictions. One minute of future happiness will infinitely reward you for all your sufferings.'

She said a lot more in a similar vein. She also reiterated her great love for Mrs Bargrave, who began to weep under such an onslaught of kind regard. They talked about many more things and Mrs Veal entreated Mrs Bargrave to write a letter to her brother outlining some small bequests she wanted to make. Mrs Bargrave rose to fetch a pen and paper but her visitor asked her to wait till she had gone. In order to change the subject, Mrs Bargrave complemented Mrs Veal on her gown, which she was told was 'of a scoured silk, newly made up'. Then the conversation turned to family matters and Mrs Bargrave suggested her friend might like to see her daughter again. Mrs Veal assented and she nipped next door to ask a neighbour to fetch her daughter for her. When she returned she was surprised to find Mrs Veal on the doorstep, ready to leave.

Asked why she had suddenly decided to go in such a hurry, Mrs Veal replied that she was expected at her cousins, the Watsons, but that Mrs Bargrave could visit her there soon. Mrs Bargrave watched her friend walk away until a turning hid her from view. The time was now 1.45pm.

The next day Mrs Bargrave sent a note to the Watson household inquiring after Mrs Veal but received the reply that they had not seen her, nor were they expecting her. So startled was Mrs Bargrave by this communication that she immediately went round to see them, despite being unacquainted with them. The puzzled Mrs Watson greeted her with scant courtesy and an argument began to brew. But just then Captain Watson returned home and he brought with him some shocking news. He had just been informed

that Mrs Veal was dead and that she had died on 7
September at noon – exactly twenty-four hours before her
apparent visit to Mrs Bargrave!

The only proof Mrs Bargrave could give of her
extraordinary experience was the information about the
gown Mrs Veal had been wearing. Mrs Watson had helped
make it and only she knew that the silk had been scoured.
Details of the minor bequests also showed intimate
knowledge Mrs Bargrave could not possibly have known.
The strange tale became a nationwide sensation.